CORNERSTONES OF FREEDOM™

THE ATTACK ON PEARL HARBOR

BY PETER BENOIT

WITHDRAWN

CHILDREN'S PRESS®
An Imprint of Scholastic Inc.
New York   Toronto   London   Auckland   Sydney
Mexico City   New Delhi   Hong Kong
Danbury, Connecticut

BRINGING HISTORY to LIFE

Content Consultant
James Marten, PhD
Professor and Chair, History Department
Marquette University
Milwaukee, Wisconsin

Library of Congress Cataloging-in-Publication Data

Benoit, Peter, 1955–
  The attack on Pearl Harbor/by Peter Benoit.
      p. cm.—(Cornerstones of freedom)
  Includes bibliographical references and index.
  ISBN 978-0-531-23601-7 (lib. bdg.)—ISBN 978-0-531-21959-1 (pbk.)
  1. Pearl Harbor (Hawaii), Attack on, 1941—Juvenile literature. I. Title.
  D767.92.B44 2013
  940.54'26693—dc23   2012030352

Photographs © 2013: Alamy Images: 46 (Tami Kauakea Winston/Photo
Resource Hawaii), 7 (War Archive); AP Images: 55 (C.P. Gorry), 54 (Joe
Rosenthal), 49 (National Park Service), 44 (U.S. Signal Corps); 2, 3, 5
bottom, 6, 10, 16, 18, 19, 23, 26, 28, 30, 32, 45, 48, 50, 57 top, 58; Denver
Public Library: 47; Getty Images: 4 top, 14 (Alinari Archives, Florence), 22
(Central Press), back cover, 5 top, 35, 59 (Express), 12 (Hulton Archive),
34 (Keystone), 13, 56 (Keystone-France/Gamma-Keystone), 33 (MPI),
20 (New York Times Co.), 29 (Thomas D. McAvoy/Time & Life Pictures);
National Archives and Records Administration: 36 (ARC Identifier 295990),
42 (Department of the Interior/ARC Identifier 520053), 37 (Franklin D.
Roosevelt Library/ARC Identifier 195617); Naval History and Heritage
Command/U.S. Navy Photograph: cover, 39, 40; Newscom/EyePress News:
17; REX USA/Victor Console/Daily Mail: 8; SuperStock, Inc.: 11, 57 bottom
(Classic Vision/age fotostock), 4 bottom, 27 (Underwood Photo Archives),
24 (Universal Images Group); The Image Works/Scherl/SZ Photo: 15.

Did you know that studying history can be fun?

BRING HISTORY TO LIFE by becoming a history investigator. Examine the evidence (primary and secondary source materials); cross-examine the people and witnesses. Take a look at what was happening at the time—but be careful! What happened years ago might suddenly become incredibly interesting and change the way you think!

Contents

Rising Tensions

Chuichi Nagumo commanded the Japanese forces in the attack on Pearl Harbor.

It was November 1941, and tension between Japan and the United States was very high. Japan had forcefully expanded into China and Vietnam, and was expressing

THE NAVAL BASE AT PEARL

interest in pushing farther into Southeast Asia. Such expansion would threaten U.S. **economic** interests in the Philippines and other parts of Southeast Asia. In addition, Japan had allied itself with Germany, which was waging war with several U.S. allies in Europe. With **diplomatic** efforts between the United States and Japan failing, war seemed inevitable.

On November 26, six aircraft carriers under the command of Japanese vice admiral Chuichi Nagumo set out from Hitokappu Bay, on the east coast of Japan. They headed in the direction of Oahu, Hawaii, home of the Pearl Harbor U.S. Naval Base. The resulting conflict would change the world forever.

Japanese forces launched their attack from Hitokappu Bay.

HARBOR WAS ESTABLISHED IN 1908.

CHAPTER 1

AN INTERNATIONAL EVENT

World leaders met in Versailles, France, in June 1919 to sign the treaty that officially ended World War I.

AT THE CONCLUSION OF WORLD War I (1914–1918), the Treaty of Versailles required Germany to give up more than one-eighth of its European territory and its **colonies** in Africa. The treaty also ordered Germany to pay **reparations** for damage it had caused the victorious Allied nations during the war. The amount was set at roughly $33 billion.

This enormous debt and loss of land contributed to the rise of the Nazi Party in Germany. The party was led by a man named Adolf Hitler. Many Germans believed that they had been treated unfairly by the Treaty of Versailles. Hitler used these feelings to gain political power, claiming that he would restore the nation to its former glory. By 1933, he had become chancellor of Germany.

Trouble in Europe

Fueled by renewed national pride and a desire to reverse the territorial losses imposed by the Treaty of Versailles, Germany began aiming to conquer surrounding nations. In 1938, Germany **annexed** Austria, which was located along the country's southern border. Other European nations allowed this to happen with almost no response. Soon afterward, it became clear that Hitler was planning to annex a portion of Czechoslovakia as well. Hoping to appease Hitler, France, Italy, and Great Britain signed the Munich Agreement with Germany. This agreement promised that the other nations would not prevent Germany from

Adolf Hitler salutes German troops as they march in Vienna, Austria, in 1938.

taking the territory. The leaders of these nations hoped that the agreement would allow them to avoid war with Germany and keep Germany from expanding more.

However, the agreement failed to slow German expansion. To make matters worse, Germany negotiated a pact with the Soviet Union in August 1939. The two countries agreed to avoid armed conflict with each other or intervention in their wars with other countries. Germany and the Soviet Union invaded Poland on September 1, 1939.

SPOTLIGHT ON

Adolf Hitler

After serving in the German army during World War I, Adolf Hitler began a political career in 1919. His Nazi political party quickly rose to power by blaming the country's problems on foreign enemies. Once Hitler had firmly established control over the country, he began planning to expand into neighboring countries.

By expanding, Hitler hoped to take control of foreign food supplies, ensuring that Germany would not suffer the food shortages that it had experienced during World War I. However, doing so would starve the residents of these foreign nations. He justified his policy of expansion by calling the foreign peoples *untermenschen,* or "subhuman."

Germany attacked from the west, while the Soviets invaded from the east, splitting Poland in two. In spring 1940, Germany continued its expansion by seizing

German forces invaded Belgium and several other European nations in early 1940.

Norway and Denmark. Later in the year, German forces unleashed an attack on France, Belgium, Luxembourg, and the Netherlands.

By June, Hitler had subdued most of Europe except for Great Britain. British Prime Minister Winston Churchill spoke before the House of Commons on May 13, 1940, about the struggle facing the nation. In the speech, Churchill pledged to serve his country with "blood, toil, tears, and sweat." Hitler responded by bombing Britain and attacking its supply ships.

CHURCHILL'S SPEECH BEFORE THE HOUSE OF COMMONS

Winston Churchill's May 13, 1940, speech before the House of Commons encouraged British citizens in the darkest days of the war while preparing them for "long months of struggle and suffering." See page 60 for a link to read and listen to the speech online.

Despite Germany's aggression toward these U.S. allies, the United States did not rush into war. The nation was still recovering from the economic disaster of the Great Depression, and President Franklin D. Roosevelt knew the American people would not back a decision to go to war.

Winston Churchill's "blood, toil, tears, and sweat" speech raised the spirits of the British people.

The Axis Forms

In September 1940, Germany, Italy, and Japan signed the Tripartite Pact. This pact guaranteed that the three nations would act as one if the United States should enter the war. Together, the three nations would come to be known as the Axis powers, while their opponents were called the Allied powers. U.S. leaders had been keeping close tabs on Japan's activities since it invaded China in 1931. After the signing of the Tripartite Pact, President Roosevelt knew that going to war either in Europe or against Japan meant fighting on two **fronts**. However, he also feared that Great Britain would be defeated. In response, he approved the Lend-Lease program in March 1941, which allowed the United States to send food and weapons to its British allies.

Representatives from Japan and Italy met with Hitler in Berlin, Germany, to sign the Tripartite Pact.

German forces (above) attacked the Soviet Union in June 1941.

Disregarding the 1939 nonaggression pact that Germany had signed with the Soviet Union, Hitler ordered an invasion of Soviet territory in June 1941. Angered at Germany's actions, Soviet leader Joseph Stalin agreed to help with Great Britain's defense.

U.S. support of Britain grew stronger throughout the summer. Roosevelt sent troops to Iceland to secure Britain's aircraft base and keep a critical supply route open. He warned German naval vessels to not patrol the western Atlantic Ocean. In September, he gave permission to U.S. warships to attack German ships that ignored the warning.

Chinese troops attempt to defend the Marco Polo Bridge against Japanese attackers.

Conflict in Asia

In July 1937, tensions between Chinese and Japanese troops boiled over at the Marco Polo Bridge outside the city of Beijing, China. For some time, Japan had been trying to purchase land next to the bridge from the Chinese government in order to build an airport. Japanese control of the bridge and nearby lands would have isolated Beijing from the rest of China. Additional Chinese forces were called in when the Japanese army began to conduct military exercises near the bridge. Tempers flared, and the two armies battled for control of the strategic point.

China and Japan soon plunged into full-scale war. Japan moved quickly and captured several Chinese cities. The **campaign** caused an outcry in the United States, Great Britain, and the Soviet Union. For decades, these nations had enjoyed free trade with China. They feared that Japanese invasion would end this profitable situation. Opposition strengthened further when Japanese troops entered Nanking in December 1937. There, they viciously assaulted Chinese **civilians**, killing between 100,000 and 300,000 people.

Japan pressed on relentlessly, and the Chinese army

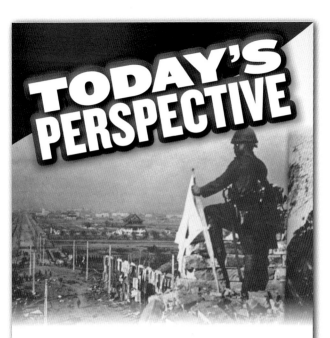

TODAY'S PERSPECTIVE

Few events have been as divisive as the Nanking massacre. It is viewed very differently in Japan than in China. Japanese historians and political figures, in an effort to build national pride, have downplayed the massacre. The general who commanded Japan's forces at Nanking is even honored at Tokyo's Yasukuni Shrine.

Similarly, China's leaders sometimes exaggerate the number of people killed at Nanking to stir patriotism. The purposes of both nations are served by promoting extreme views of the event. Perspective has even changed in the United States. The massacre stirred considerable sympathy for the Chinese people in 1937. After World War II, however, the United States needed Japan as an ally and often ignored the event's bloody details.

continually retreated. However, ceaseless war against China soon began to drain Japan's resources. By 1940, Japanese leaders had begun to realize that it was impossible to impose military control over all of China. They began to chart a different course. Japanese prime minister Fumimaro Konoe promoted an economic alliance, named the Greater East Asia Co-Prosperity Sphere, among China, Manchuria, Japan, and parts of Southeast Asia.

Fumimaro Konoe became prime minister of Japan in 1937.

The United States held territory in the Philippines.

The economic plan thinly masked Japan's desire to control the resources of Southeast Asia. It was meant to rid Asia of colonial outposts controlled by the United States and Great Britain. U.S. leaders viewed the economic plan as a veiled threat against U.S. territory in the Philippines. If Japan were allowed to take control of Southeast Asia's resources, it would be able to fuel its powerful war machine. Roosevelt was in an impossible position. Believing war was inevitable, he would have to convince the American people that no other course would preserve their freedom.

CHAPTER 2

AMERICA'S DILEMMA

President Roosevelt hoped that economic pressure would slow the rapid expansion of the Axis powers.

NBC

WGN

CBS

PRESIDENT ROOSEVELT FEARED

that the Axis powers would soon control a large part of the world if no action were taken against them. As early as October 1937, he called on nations around the world to apply economic pressure to "**quarantine**" the enemy nations.

Critics of this policy pointed out that the United States might be pulled into wars on two fronts. This would be an unwelcome position for a nation still recovering from the Great Depression. Polls suggested that the American people strongly supported sending aid to China and Great Britain, even if they wished to avoid war. U.S. leaders wondered if providing assistance to China would bring the United States closer to war with Japan. However, many believed that neglecting to help China would make Japan an even more powerful foe.

The Kwantung Army fought during Japan's war with China.

Inching Toward War

Germany's invasion of the Soviet Union in June 1941 also pushed the United States and Japan closer to war. With its hopes for an alliance with both Germany and the Soviets denied, Japan contemplated an attack on the Soviet Union despite the neutrality treaty they had signed two months earlier. Japanese leaders were drawn to the plan. They believed that the Soviet army, with resources stretched thin by war on two fronts, could eventually be defeated. However, Japan's Kwantung Army, based in Manchuria, would require supplies—and time—before the plan could be executed.

A FIRSTHAND LOOK AT
ROOSEVELT'S "QUARANTINE" SPEECH

On October 5, 1937, President Roosevelt spoke in Chicago, Illinois, calling on democratic societies to "quarantine" aggressor nations. This was an important first step away from policies of nonintervention. See page 60 for a link to read Roosevelt's speech online.

In recognition of these uncertainties, Japan's navy pressed for a campaign in Southeast Asia. Going south offered many advantages. Japan's invasion of the northern part of French Indochina (now Laos, Cambodia, and Vietnam) the previous July had not been widely protested. Extending influence in the region would likely be met with little resistance from the Allies.

Japan had a powerful navy during World War II.

Possession of Indochina would bring Japan closer to realizing its plan for a Greater East Asia Co-Prosperity Sphere. It would also place vast resources of oil, rubber, and tin at the country's disposal. All of that would be necessary to support Japan's war goals.

U.S. leaders saw Japan's decision to go south as a dangerous development. If Japan commanded Indochina's resources, it would be a much stronger foe. Furthermore, a successful Japanese campaign there posed an imminent danger to the Philippines, Dutch East Indies, and the nearby British colonies of Malaya and Burma. The conquest of these colonies would

Many British people lived in Malaya and Burma in the years leading up to World War II.

isolate New Zealand and Australia, and defending them would split Britain's resources and weaken its defenses at home.

Economic Warfare

In reaction to the threat, the United States and Great Britain froze Japanese **assets**, requiring Japanese businessmen to secure the approval of U.S. and British leaders to release funds held in those nations' banks. The move placed heavy pressure on Japan. It could no longer import oil from the

A VIEW FROM ABR★AD

Congress passed the Tydings-McDuffie Act in 1934. The act promised independence to the Philippines in 1946. However, Filipinos were alarmed when Japanese expansion continued and the United States finalized a war plan that prioritized the defense of European allies. Filipino leaders envisioned the islands overrun by Japanese forces, their homeland turned into a vast battlefield. Consequently, Filipinos considered it a mixed blessing when General Douglas MacArthur was appointed commander of U.S.-Philippine forces and America's military presence was expanded in the area. Independence seemed further away, but the alternative was worse.

United States. Without oil, it would be difficult for Japan to move against the Soviet Union. Japanese leaders would also have to reconsider aggression in Southeast Asia. At the same time, the United States would continue to provide aid to the Chinese.

Hirohito served as emperor of Japan from 1926 until his death in 1989.

By August 1941, hostilities had risen to a dangerous level. The United States, Australia, Great Britain, and the Netherlands had all ceased selling oil, iron ore, and steel to Japan. With supplies required for war efforts dwindling and their economy smothered, many Japanese believed that the Western powers were bent on Japan's destruction. At a September 6 meeting led by Emperor Hirohito and Prime Minister Konoe, Japan resolved to wage war against the United States.

However, Japan had serious materials shortages. So even as the country prepared for war, it opened negotiations with the United States. Its government demanded that the United States cease support of China and resume trade with Japan. The United States wanted to see some of Japan's troops withdrawn from China. The two nations were unable to reach an agreement. Because a showdown with Germany might occur any day, President Roosevelt continued negotiations with Japan as the United States prepared for war in Europe.

Japanese representatives met with U.S. Secretary of State Cordell Hull (center) on November 17, 1941, to discuss options for peace between the nations.

Planning the Attack

Prime Minister Konoe grew frustrated as fruitless negotiations dragged on. He resigned on October 16. Hideki Tōjō, already serving as war minister, replaced him. Speaking to Joseph Grew, America's **ambassador** in Tokyo, Tōjō stressed Emperor Hirohito's desire to preserve peace. Negotiations were renewed but with little hope of success. About two weeks later, on November 2,

Hideki Tōjō replaced Fumimaro Konoe as prime minister of Japan.

Hirohito consented to war. Japanese military commanders set about making a detailed plan for an attack on the U.S. Navy at Pearl Harbor. They shared this plan with Hirohito on November 8.

For months, Japan had gathered detailed information about Pearl Harbor from spies who moved freely throughout Oahu. But American intelligence relied on intercepting coded diplomatic messages, none of which had direct bearing on the plans for attack. Reports from American **reconnaissance** planes and ships all pointed to the Japanese fleet moving toward Indochina. These reports would soon prove to be fatally misleading.

TODAY'S PERSPECTIVE

In the wake of the Pearl Harbor attack, the United States mobilized in response to what was declared a "sneak attack." This emotionally loaded phrase stirred American patriotism as the nation prepared for war. However, historians now say it was not so much a sneak attack as a critical intelligence failure. U.S. military leaders thought that Japan might attack the Philippines. Information from airplane reconnaissance and traffic analysis, though incomplete, supported this belief. Those leaders believed the Japanese were inferior and incapable of carrying out an attack on Pearl Harbor. This turned out to be a disastrous error.

CHAPTER 3

TORA! TORA! TORA!

Before the 1941 attack, Pearl Harbor was the United States' main naval base in the Pacific Ocean.

IN THE DAYS LEADING UP TO the attack on Pearl Harbor, American military commanders knew that war could erupt at any moment. As the center of U.S. Navy activity in the Pacific Ocean, Pearl Harbor would be an important strategic point if combat broke out.

Navy intelligence reports could not account for the locations of several Japanese fleet carriers known to have been in the area. However, such gaps were not uncommon. These same carriers had gone unaccounted for on a dozen other occasions in the previous six months. It concerned America's military leaders more that the Japanese navy had changed its communication signals, making it more difficult to track its movements.

H. E. Kimmel was in charge of the U.S. naval forces at Pearl Harbor.

Making Mistakes

To complicate matters further, Admiral H. E. Kimmel, commander in chief of the U.S. Pacific Fleet, had failed to respond appropriately to an order on November 27. He had been told to place his ships in a standard defensive arrangement, which called for battleships to patrol farther out from the base. Instead, Kimmel continued to focus patrols on the waters surrounding Pearl Harbor. As a result, the fleet was on low-level alert.

Admiral Kimmel decided to keep American battleships in the harbor because few aircraft carriers were available to provide airplanes for defense. The carriers *Lexington*, *Enterprise*, and *Saratoga* had been sent elsewhere. Kimmel considered an attack on Pearl Harbor unlikely, but he believed that local army aircraft would provide enough protection if such an attack did occur. However, senior U.S. Army commander Walter Short feared that enemy spies would sabotage the aircraft. He ordered aircraft to be set out in neat rows and aircraft ammunition to be locked away. At the same time these critical errors and communication failures were weakening American defenses, the detailed Japanese war plan had already been set in motion.

Walter Short's fear of sabotage led to U.S. aircraft at Pearl Harbor being arranged in a way that made them easily targeted by enemy aircraft.

That plan depended on the expertise of Japanese naval aviators Mitsuo Fuchida and Minoru Genda, as well as other senior commanders. The plan had two major goals: destroying U.S. aircraft carriers and sinking battleships. It was to be executed by a six-carrier strike force. Other fleets would support the strike force with airplanes, ships, and submarines. Once the strike force arrived 200 miles (322 kilometers) north of Oahu, two planes would scout the defenses of Pearl Harbor and send reports as preparations moved into the final phase.

Mitsuo Fuchida famously shouted "Tora! Tora! Tora!" into his microphone as the Japanese forces came upon Pearl Harbor. This was a code word that meant to start the attack.

The Attack Begins

By 3:30 a.m. on December 7, Japanese pilots were preparing for their deadly mission. Three hours later, the first wave of dive-bombers, torpedo bombers, and fighter planes was in the air and streaking toward Oahu. At Pearl Harbor, many U.S. servicemen slept late, anticipating another peaceful Sunday morning. Others were eating a leisurely breakfast. Japan's strike force commanders were surprised to find the U.S. fleet resting quietly. Realizing that the attack would be completely unexpected, Mitsuo Fuchida transmitted his findings to the strike force commanders by shouting the code word *tora*.

YESTERDAY'S HEADLINES

New York World-Telegram

1500 DEAD IN HAWAII

Congress Votes War on Japan; Manila Bases Bombed Again

As the United States prepared for war, sensational newspaper headlines and accounts of the Pearl Harbor attack served two purposes. They expressed a nation's outrage and gave focus and new purpose to a nation that had avoided military intervention in the conflict in Europe. In the months leading up to the Pearl Harbor attack, polls suggested that Americans increasingly favored entering the war. President Roosevelt, sensing the likelihood of war in advance, had approved a huge military spending bill in 1940. After the Pearl Harbor attack, the nation joined together in support of the war.

The U.S. battleship *Oklahoma* was knocked onto its side by Japanese torpedoes.

Japanese fighter planes attacked rows of aircraft at several U.S. military installations as they flew over the island. Dive-bombers soon joined the strike force's fighters. Flying below rooftop level, they dropped torpedoes into the water. The harbor's eight battleships felt the full fury of the Japanese assault.

Because Pearl Harbor had been on low-level alert, only a few manned machine guns, particularly those on the battleship *Nevada*, fought back at the first strike. They were able to shoot down enemy torpedo planes. Other U.S. battleships did not fare so well. The *Oklahoma* was hit by four torpedoes. It turned on its side with only its hull protruding from the water. The *West Virginia* tilted dangerously. The worst was yet to come. Fuchida directed his high-level bombers, with their armor-piercing bombs, to join the attack on the battleships. Within minutes, the *Maryland*, *Tennessee*, *West Virginia*, and *Arizona* had all sustained heavy damage.

The *Arizona* was hit at least five times. One bomb ripped through the battleship's two armored decks before detonating. A powerful explosion rocked the harbor as flames erupted from the *Arizona*. Thick black smoke filled the sky. Dead and dying men lay on the deck. The living stepped over charred bodies to assist the wounded as shrapnel whistled by them. Others

The *Arizona* sank in a cloud of smoke.

were injured and thrown into the harbor by the force of the explosion. They struggled to swim away from the doomed battleship. The *Arizona* split open and sank to the muddy bottom of the harbor, carrying with it more than 1,100 crewmen. It broke the water main leading to Ford Island, dealing a fatal blow to firefighting efforts. Oil pouring from the doomed battleship caught fire and turned the harbor into an inferno.

Debris and charred corpses littered the disabled *Tennessee*, now threatened by the burning oil. Crewmen fired jets of water from the ship to keep the flaming oil at bay. The sunken *West Virginia* blocked the efforts of the *Tennessee*'s crew to move the ship from the surrounding dangers. As U.S. crewmen struggled against impossible odds, Japanese fighters flew low and fired their guns until the smoke from the burning oil made further passes unproductive. The attack began to slow by 8:30 a.m., but it was far from over. During a brief lull before the second wave of the attack, U.S. pilots worked feverishly to fuel and arm P-40 fighter planes.

The Second Wave

Fuchida directed the second wave of the attack to begin. Bomber planes retraced the path of the first attack, striking ships and dockyards. In the harbor itself, the 34,000-ton *Nevada* had worked up steam and backed out of the surrounding wreckage. The giant ship moved across the harbor toward the main channel, which led out to sea. This raised another danger for the U.S.

Although the *Nevada* avoided blocking the main channel out of Pearl Harbor, where it could have been sunk, it still took heavy damage during the attack.

fleet. If bombers sunk the *Nevada* in Pearl Harbor's main channel, the entire fleet would be blocked for months and the Japanese navy would achieve its war aims without opposition. As bombers descended on the battleship, a strategic order came down from the signal tower: "Stay clear of channel." The *Nevada*'s crew followed the orders and gently grounded the ship along the muddy coast.

Japanese bombers turned their attention to the battleship *Pennsylvania* and the destroyers *Cassin*, *Shaw*, and *Downes*. The *Pennsylvania* received a direct hit while the three destroyers burned nearby. By 9:30 a.m., the worst of the attack was over. Random strafing eventually ended around 9:45 a.m., when the Japanese forces withdrew.

In the aftermath of the attack, rescue boats attempted to save men from the burning ships in the harbor.

Japanese forces left behind hundreds of damaged or destroyed airplanes and ships. More than 2,300 American servicemen lay dead. Around 1,200 more were wounded, and there were around 90 civilian casualties. The Japanese losses in the raid were far less: five midget submarines, 30 aircraft, and fewer than 100 men dead. Admiral Kimmel had watched the gruesome attack from his office across the harbor, where a machine gun bullet had shattered the window and grazed his chest. In less than a week, he would be relieved of his command, the United States would be at war, and the world would never be the same.

A VIEW FROM ABR★AD

Adolf Hitler was thrilled to learn the news of Japan's attack on the U.S. fleet at Pearl Harbor. He responded by saying, "We can't lose the war at all. We now have an ally which has never been conquered in 3,000 years." Hitler's Operation Barbarossa, the invasion of the Soviet Union, had met stiff resistance. He thought that the Pearl Harbor attack would inspire the United States to make war in the Pacific its top priority. His prediction proved to be wrong, however, as the U.S. forces entered World War II with an attack on German forces in Europe. Still, Hitler was confident. The next day, he ordered German U-boats to sink U.S. ships.

CHAPTER 4

A NATION GOES TO WAR

President Roosevelt signed the declaration of war against Japan the day after the Pearl Harbor attack.

BOTH THE UNITED STATES
and Great Britain declared war on Japan shortly
after the Pearl Harbor attack. President Roosevelt
called December 7, 1941, "a date which will live
in infamy" in a December 8 speech before a
joint session of Congress. Japanese attacks on
Malaya, Singapore, and Hong Kong as well as its
torpedoing of two British ships served to further
convince the Allies that Japan was a serious threat.

In response to the U.S. declaration of war against
Japan, Germany and Italy declared war on the
United States four days later. America was now
committed to waging war in Europe and the Pacific.

Japan began bombing the Philippines almost immediately after the attack on Pearl Harbor.

Bataan and Corregidor

A few hours after the Pearl Harbor attack, Japan attacked the Philippines. Defensive forces outnumbered Japan's attacking 14th Army. However, the less-experienced Filipino fighters struggled to contain Japan's more experienced troops. The defenders, including U.S. troops, were forced to retreat to the Bataan Peninsula and Corregidor Island. By April 9, 1942, Bataan had fallen to the Japanese. Corregidor fell less than a month later.

A FIRSTHAND LOOK AT
ROOSEVELT'S PEARL HARBOR SPEECH

On December 8, 1941, President Roosevelt spoke before a joint session of Congress about the horrors of the Japanese attack on Pearl Harbor. An hour later, Congress declared war on Japan. See page 60 for a link to listen to Roosevelt's speech online.

After surrendering, the U.S. and Filipino troops at Bataan were marched 55 miles (88 km) to a Japanese prison camp. The march resulted in many deaths. Captives who fell behind were beaten and stabbed. Between 7,000 and 10,000 people died along the way.

The Bataan Death March was a horrifying ordeal for the captive U.S. and Filipino soldiers.

The Niihau Incident

In the aftermath of the Pearl Harbor attack, Japanese pilot Shigenori Nishikaichi was forced to crash-land on the nearby island of Niihau, Hawaii, when his aircraft was shot down. The privately owned island had around 180 inhabitants, including two Japanese families. None of the residents were aware that Pearl Harbor had been attacked.

A man named Howard Kaleohano was the first to arrive at the crash site. There, he took Japanese documents from the airplane. When it was determined the pilot had survived, a Japanese immigrant named Yoshio Harada and his wife were sought out to translate discussions between the pilot and islanders. Nishikaichi was placed under guard at the Haradas' home. Eventually, Nishikaichi

The burning of a village on Niihau by a Japanese immigrant, along with a Japanese fighter pilot, spurred the country's distrust of Japanese Americans.

convinced Yoshio Harada to help him recover his missing documents, and the two proceeded to set fire to the village as they searched for the papers. Nishikaichi was killed by a Niihau resident, and Harada shot himself. Harada's actions during the Niihau incident caused some people to wonder if Japanese Americans could be trusted to remain loyal to the United States.

Internment

Widespread hatred and distrust of the Japanese spread throughout the United States in the months following the Pearl Harbor attack. The media fed the hysteria and helped

TODAY'S PERSPECTIVE

Executive Order 9066, signed into law in February 1942, led to the relocation and internment of Japanese Americans. This order allowed the military to designate areas off limits to whomever it deemed necessary. Without directly stating it, this referred to Japanese Americans, who were beginning to be viewed as a threat.

In 1942, Colorado Governor Ralph L. Carr (above) stood alone when he dared to publicly apologize to Japanese Americans for internment. As a result, he was not reelected to office. Years later, in 1976, President Gerald Ford called internment a "national mistake." In 1988, President Ronald Reagan signed the Civil Liberties Act. This act paid a total of $1.6 billion to survivors of the internment camps.

Lieutenant General John L. DeWitt (left) encouraged negative feelings about Japanese Americans in the United States.

to spread **stereotypes**. Some anti-Japanese groups printed fake hunting licenses that declared "open season" on the Japanese. By 1944, polls indicated that between 10 and 13 percent of all Americans favored exterminating all the Japanese.

Government officials such as Lieutenant General John L. DeWitt argued that Japanese Americans were a national security threat. California attorney general Earl Warren began a campaign to place people of Japanese heritage in internment camps. On February 19, 1942, President Roosevelt signed Executive Order 9066 into law. This new law granted military commanders the power to exclude Japanese Americans from designated military areas.

On March 18, Roosevelt created the War Relocation Authority. This group oversaw 10 internment camps that held 120,000 Japanese Americans in seven states. Some Japanese Americans were given as few as six days to get their affairs in order before moving to the camps. They were forced to sell their property and possessions, and their bank accounts were frozen. The living conditions in internment camps were horrific. There was neither plumbing nor stoves for cooking food. Armed guards sometimes shot people who dared to wander outside the

Internment camps were fenced in and heavily guarded.

fenced-in compound. Such interment camps continued to operate until 1945, when the war was almost over.

Such negative feelings about the Japanese would eventually make the 1945 atomic bombings of Hiroshima and Nagasaki more acceptable to the American public. President Harry S. Truman wrote of the bombings that, "When you have to deal with a beast you have to treat him as a beast."

The government's right to detain citizens would be challenged at the U.S. Supreme Court level in the years following the Pearl Harbor attack. In many of the legal

A U.S. atomic bomb reduced the Japanese city of Hiroshima to rubble.

cases, the court chose to uphold the logic of internment. In the 21st century, these cases have been cited to justify the expansion of government powers during the "war on terror."

The same type of violent thoughts aimed at Japanese Americans during World War II were later focused on Arab Americans after the terrorist attacks of September 11, 2001. Many Arab Americans were accused of being terrorists. Fake "terrorist hunting licenses" began appearing in 2001. They bore frightening similarities to the "permits" declaring "open season" on the Japanese six decades earlier. Unfortunately, fear and prejudice are parts of the December 7, 1941, legacy that live on today.

A VIEW FROM ABROAD

U.S. **propaganda** during the war depicted the Japanese as violent, sneaky enemies who should not be trusted. They were believed to be enslaving or murdering Chinese civilians. U.S. propaganda pointed to the "sneak attack" at Pearl Harbor and the extreme violence of the attack on Nanking as evidence of Japanese ruthlessness.

Japanese propaganda, on the other hand, depicted U.S. soldiers as weak people who could never defeat the Japanese. It also claimed that the United States was fighting mainly to protect its economic interests in Asia. Japanese officials presented the coming war against the United States as a battle of liberation against a colonial oppressor.

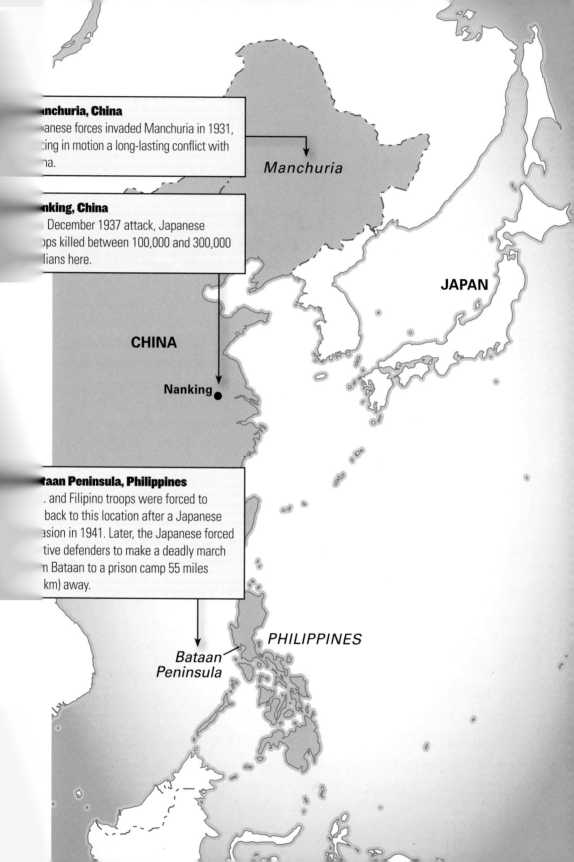

...nchuria, China
...anese forces invaded Manchuria in 1931,
...ing in motion a long-lasting conflict with
...na.

Manchuria

...nking, China
... December 1937 attack, Japanese
...ps killed between 100,000 and 300,000
...lians here.

JAPAN

CHINA

Nanking

...taan Peninsula, Philippines
... and Filipino troops were forced to
... back to this location after a Japanese
...sion in 1941. Later, the Japanese forced
...tive defenders to make a deadly march
...n Bataan to a prison camp 55 miles
...km) away.

PHILIPPINES

*Bataan
Peninsula*

MAP OF THE EVENTS
What Happened Where?

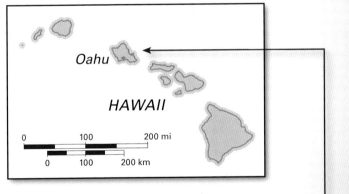

Oahu

HAWAII

| 0 | 100 | 200 mi |
| 0 | 100 | 200 km |

Oahu Island, Hawaii
This island was home to the Pearl Harbor
U.S. Naval Base. Since 1962, it has been a
national memorial.

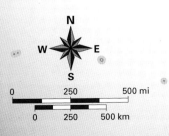

N
W   E
S

| 0 | 250 | 500 mi |
| 0 | 250 | 500 km |

A Lasting Legacy

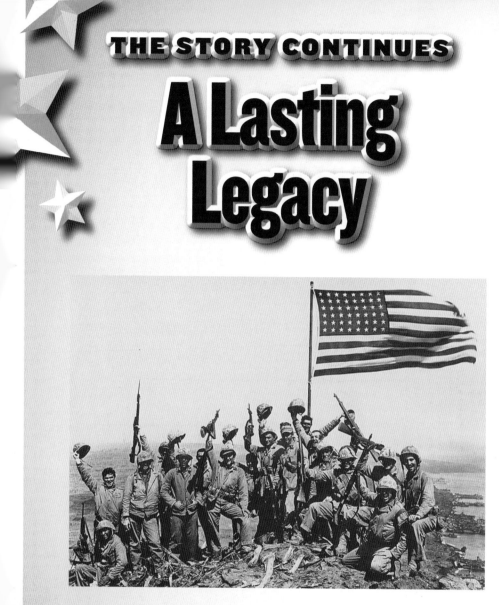

U.S. forces were largely successful in their attacks on Japan.

Although Japan caused significant damage to Pearl Harbor, it failed to destroy its main intended targets. U.S. aircraft carriers and fuel supplies at Pearl Harbor remained intact after the attack. This allowed the U.S.

BETWEEN 40 AND 50 MILLION PEOPLE

forces to achieve a devastating victory against Japan in the Battle of Midway several months later.

The attack on Pearl Harbor elevated American patriotism, but it also revealed the fault lines in U.S. society. The attack uncovered the limitations of U.S. intelligence gathering on the eve of the nation's entrance into the war and the vulnerability of its Pacific Fleet. While American soldiers fought for life and liberty, the media fanned the flames of hatred. Political leaders violated the rights of Japanese American citizens to satisfy their fear. As the United States' strength was confirmed in the aftermath of Pearl Harbor, so was its vulnerability.

Japanese officials signed surrender documents aboard a U.S. ship on September 2, 1945. General Douglas MacArthur (left, standing at microphone) presided over the event.

WERE KILLED IN WORLD WAR II.

Winston Churchill

Winston Churchill (1874–1965) was the British prime minister during World War II. He strengthened the resolve of his countrymen in their nation's darkest hour.

Joseph Stalin (1879–1953) was the Soviet premier from 1941 to 1953. He instituted an extensive economic policy to industrialize his nation.

John L. DeWitt (1880–1962) was a U.S. lieutenant general who was a vocal supporter of Japanese American internment during World War II.

Douglas MacArthur (1880–1964) was a U.S. general who returned to active duty in July 1941 to lead the Philippine army in preparation for an anticipated Japanese attack.

Franklin D. Roosevelt (1882–1945) was the 32nd president whose unflagging optimism steadied the nation through the depths of the Great Depression and the dangers of World War II.

H. E. Kimmel (1882–1968) was commander in chief of the U.S. Pacific Fleet during the attack on Pearl Harbor. He failed to recognize the likelihood of imminent attack on the Oahu base and take appropriate action.

Hideki Tōjō (1884–1948) was prime minister of Japan at the time of the Pearl Harbor attack. He was directly responsible for the attack.

Hideki Tōjō

Chuichi Nagumo (1886–1944) was a vice admiral in the Imperial Japanese Navy and a commander of the strike force at Pearl Harbor.

Adolf Hitler (1889–1945) was German chancellor from 1933 to 1945 and head of the Nazi Party during World War II. His policies fueled Germany's aggressive expansion.

Adolf Hitler

1931

The Japanese army invades Manchuria.

1933

Adolf Hitler is named chancellor of Germany.

1940

September
Germany, Italy, and Japan sign the Tripartite Pact.

1941

June
Germany invades the Soviet Union.

August
The Allies initiate an oil embargo on Japan.

October
Hideki Tōjō is named Japan's prime minister.

December 7
The Imperial Japanese Navy attacks Pearl Harbor.

December 8
The United States and Great Britain declare war on Japan.

1937

July
The Marco Polo Bridge incident worsens relations between Japan and China.

October
President Franklin Roosevelt delivers his "Quarantine Speech" in Chicago.

December
Hundreds of thousands of Chinese civilians are killed in the Nanking massacre.

1939

September
Germany and the Soviet Union invade Poland.

1942

February 19
President Franklin Roosevelt signs Executive Order 9066 into law.

March 18
President Roosevelt creates the War Relocation Authority.

1988

The U.S. government pays $1.6 billion to internment camp survivors.

New York World-Telegram   7TH SPORTS

1500 DEAD IN HAWAII
Congress Votes War on Japan; Manila Bases Bombed Again

Navy Enlistment Office Swamped by Volunteers

Britain Declares War on Japan

LIVING HISTORY

Primary sources provide firsthand evidence about a topic. Witnesses to a historical event create primary sources. They include autobiographies, newspaper reports of the time, oral histories, photographs, and memoirs. A secondary source analyzes primary sources, and is one step or more removed from the event. Secondary sources include textbooks, encyclopedias, and commentaries. To view the following primary and secondary sources, go to www.factsfornow.scholastic.com. Enter the keywords **Pearl Harbor** and look for the Living History logo ⚡.

⚡ **Admiral Kimmel's Testimony** Watch a video excerpt of Admiral H. E. Kimmel's testimony before a congressional committee about his preparations for the Pearl Harbor attack.

⚡ **Churchill's Speech Before the House of Commons** Read or listen to Winston Churchill's first speech before the House of Commons, encouraging British citizens in the darkest days of the war while preparing them for "long months of struggle and suffering."

⚡ **Roosevelt's Pearl Harbor Speech** Hear President Franklin Roosevelt's December 8, 1941, speech before a joint session of Congress about the horrors of the Japanese attack on Pearl Harbor the previous day.

⚡ **Roosevelt's "Quarantine" Speech** Read President Roosevelt's October 5, 1937, speech, which called on democratic societies to "quarantine" aggressor nations. This was a first but important step away from policies of nonintervention.

RESOURCES

Books

Adams, Simon. *World War II*. New York: DK Publishing, 2007.

Chrisp, Peter. *World War II: Fighting For Freedom*. New York: Scholastic Reference, 2010.

Dougherty, Steve. *Pearl Harbor: The U.S. Enters World War II*. New York: Franklin Watts, 2010.

Grant, R.G. *World War II: The Events and Their Impact on Real People*. New York: DK Publishing, 2008.

Sakurai, Gail. *Japanese American Internment Camps*. New York: Children's Press, 2002.

Visit this Scholastic Web site for more information on Pearl Harbor: www.factsfornow.scholastic.com Enter the keywords Pearl Harbor

GLOSSARY

ambassador (am-BAS-uh-dur) a person sent by a government to represent it in a foreign country

annexed (AN-ekst) took control of a country or territory by force

assets (AS-ets) valuable things that a person or business owns

campaign (kam-PAYN) organized action in order to achieve a particular goal

civilians (suh-VIL-yuhnz) people who are not members of the armed forces

colonies (KAH-luh-neez) territories that have been settled by people from another country and are controlled by that country

diplomatic (dip-luh-MAT-ik) having to do with relationships between countries

economic (ek-uh-NAH-mik) of or having to do with the system of buying, selling, and making things in a place

fronts (FRUHNTS) areas where two armies meet and fight

propaganda (prah-puh-GAN-duh) information that is spread to influence the way people think, to gain supporters, or to damage an opposing group

quarantine (KWOR-uhn-teen) keep something apart from other things or people in order to prevent it from spreading

reconnaissance (rih-KAHN-uh-suhns) activities used to gain knowledge of enemy plans or tactics

reparations (rep-uh-RAY-shuhnz) payments made by a defeated nation in order to make up for damages caused during a war

stereotypes (STER-ee-oh-tipes) widely held but overly simple ideas, opinions, or images of a person, group, or thing

Page numbers in *italics* indicate illustrations.

ABOUT THE AUTHOR

Peter Benoit is a graduate of Skidmore College in Saratoga Springs, New York. His degree is in mathematics. He is the author of dozens of Children's Press books, with topics as diverse as Native Americans, ecosystems, disasters, American history, and ancient civilizations.